GAME ON!

Animal Crossing

JESSICA RUSICK

Checkerboard
Library

An Imprint of Abdo Publishing
abdobooks.com

abdobooks.com

Published by Abdo Publishing, a division of ABDO, PO Box 398166, Minneapolis, Minnesota 55439. Copyright © 2022 by Abdo Consulting Group, Inc. International copyrights reserved in all countries. No part of this book may be reproduced in any form without written permission from the publisher. Checkerboard Library™ is a trademark and logo of Abdo Publishing.

Printed in the United States of America, North Mankato, Minnesota
052021
092021

THIS BOOK CONTAINS
RECYCLED MATERIALS

Design: Aruna Rangarajan, Mighty Media, Inc.
Production: Mighty Media, Inc.
Editor: Rebecca Felix
Design Elements: Shutterstock Images
Cover Photograph: Shutterstock Images
Interior Photographs: ArcadeImages/Alamy, p. 24 (bottom); Brian Jiang/Flickr, p. 11; Bryan Ochalla/ Flickr, pp. 9, 17, 28 (bottom right); charming meiler/Flickr, p. 5; Dennis Amith/Flickr, pp. 21, 25 (top); Evan-Amos/Wikimedia Commons, pp. 24, 28-29 (top); Hanbyul/Flickr, p. 23; John/Flickr, p. 13; ninetailedsquid/Flickr, p. 27; Pavel Kapish/Alamy, pp. 19, 29; Redazione Fuorigio.co/Flickr, p. 15; Shutterstock Images, pp. 25, 29 (bottom); Vince Bucci/AP Images, pp. 7, 28

Library of Congress Control Number: 2020949737

Publisher's Cataloging-in-Publication Data
Names: Rusick, Jessica, author.
Title: Animal Crossing / by Jessica Rusick
Description: Minneapolis, Minnesota : Abdo Publishing, 2022 | Series: Game On! | Includes online resources and index.
Identifiers: ISBN 9781532195785 (lib. bdg.) | ISBN 9781644945476 (pbk.) | ISBN 9781098216511 (ebook)
Subjects: LCSH: Video games--Juvenile literature. | Simulation games--Juvenile literature. | Nintendo video games--Juvenile literature. | Video games and children--Juvenile literature.
Classification: DDC 794.8--dc23

NOTE TO READERS

Video games that depict shooting or other violent acts should be subject to adult discretion and awareness that exposure to such acts may affect players' perceptions of violence in the real world.

CONTENTS

ANIMAL CROSSING

A smiling human villager runs through a colorful cartoon town. On the banks of a river, the villager watches a butterfly slowly fly by. The villager's net swoops down on the bug. Hooray! He has caught a tiger butterfly. The villager gives the butterfly to a town resident, a talking frog named Tad. In return, Tad gives the villager a shirt.

Nintendo's *Animal Crossing* is a life **simulation** video game series. In *Animal Crossing* games, there are no levels to beat. There are no enemies to fight. And, the goal is not to win. Instead, players live a **virtual** life in a small community. They gather items, decorate their homes, and build relationships with the town's talking animal residents.

Animal Crossing was one of the first life simulation video games themed around friends and community. It is also one of the most popular. For decades, players have loved the *Animal Crossing* **franchise** for its fun, relaxing gameplay.

Many video games feature battles, violence, or complex gameplay. *Animal Crossing*'s simpler, more cheerful gameplay makes it appealing to a variety of people worldwide.

2

ANIMAL FOREST

Animal Crossing's creator is Katsuya Eguchi. He was born in Tokyo, Japan, in 1965. Eguchi was raised in Chiba, Japan. In 1986, he got a job working for the video game company Nintendo. Eguchi moved 500 miles (805 km) from home to work at Nintendo in Kyoto, Japan.

Eguchi missed his family and friends after moving. These feelings inspired him. Eguchi wondered if he could create a video game around the ideas of family, friendship, and community. In the next years, he worked on many games for Nintendo. But Eguchi never forgot his idea.

In April 2001, Eguchi brought his idea to life. That year, *Animal Forest* **debuted** for the Nintendo 64 (N64) in Japan. Each player navigated the game as a human character who moves to a small town filled with talking animal residents. The character takes out a loan for a house from a resident named Tom Nook.

Animal Crossing creator Katsuya Eguchi. He wanted his game to mimic the experience of moving to a new place and building a life there.

Each player could also talk to the town's residents and build relationships with them. The player would collect items such as fish, bugs, and fruit for the residents. In return, the residents would gift the player items and money, called Bells. The player could use Bells to repay their loan to Nook, expand their house, and buy goods at shops.

Another feature of *Animal Forest* was real-time gameplay. At the start of the game, the player entered the date and time where they lived. This made the game's town reflect the player's real-world season and time of day.

Animal Forest was a **unique** game. And players loved it! In December 2001, an **upgraded** version of *Animal Forest* was released in Japan. It was made to play on Nintendo's new home **console**, the GameCube. The new version of the game was called *Animal Crossing*.

In September 2002, *Animal Crossing* **debuted** in the United States. In 2003 and 2004, the game debuted in Australia and Europe.

A UNIQUE TOWN

In *Animal Crossing*, players' towns were **randomly generated** by the game. So, each player's town had a different layout and residents. The chance of two players starting with the same town was very low.

Animal Crossing was largely the same as *Animal Forest*. However, *Animal Crossing* included new animal residents. It also let players **customize** clothing with their own patterns. The new game was an instant hit.

Dōbutsu no Mori was the Japanese name for *Animal Forest*. The game was originally made for the N64. But the N64 was becoming less popular by 2001, so Nintendo released *Animal Forest* on the GameCube instead.

3

WILD WORLD

In 2005, Nintendo released *Animal Crossing: Wild World* in the United States and Japan. The game released in Europe the next year. *Wild World* was made for the Nintendo DS, a handheld **console**. Unlike the GameCube, the DS was **portable**. Fans loved their new ability to take the game with them and play on the go.

Fans also loved the game's new features. In *Wild World*, players could change their character's hairstyle and hair color. There were also new residents and options to create **custom** clothing. In addition, players could cut down trees and plant flowers.

The DS could also connect to the internet. This allowed *Wild World* players to visit other people's towns. Up to three other players could join a

FLOWER FEATURE

In *Wild World*, players could plant two flowers of the same type, but different colors, next to each other. This could cause a third flower to grow in a color blended from those of the first two. For example, a red tulip next to a white one could make a pink tulip grow!

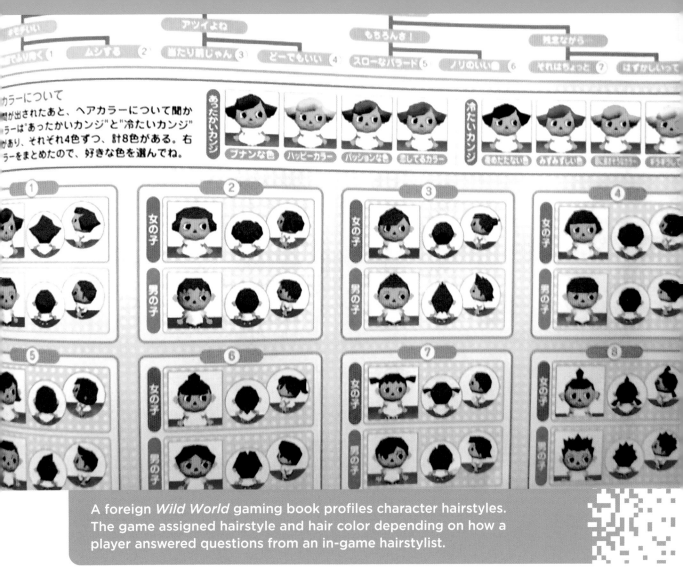

A foreign *Wild World* gaming book profiles character hairstyles. The game assigned hairstyle and hair color depending on how a player answered questions from an in-game hairstylist.

player in their town at one time! By 2009, *Wild World* had sold more than 10 million copies.

CITY FOLK

A new *Animal Crossing* game, *City Folk*, was released for the Nintendo Wii in 2008. Players could wave the Wii's motion capture remote in specific ways to use tools like fishing rods and nets. Players could also use the Wii Speak microphone **accessory** to talk to fellow gamers while visiting each other's towns.

In *City Folk*, characters still lived in small towns. However, they could visit nearby cities filled with shops. There, they could buy clothes, visit hairdressers, and talk to city residents.

By 2009, *City Folk* had sold more than 3 million copies. However, many players felt *City Folk* wasn't different enough from previous *Animal Crossing* games.

For example, many *City Folk* shops were the same as the shops in previous versions. In addition, players missed being able to play the game on a **portable console**. Because of these issues, many *Animal Crossing* fans continued to play *Wild World*

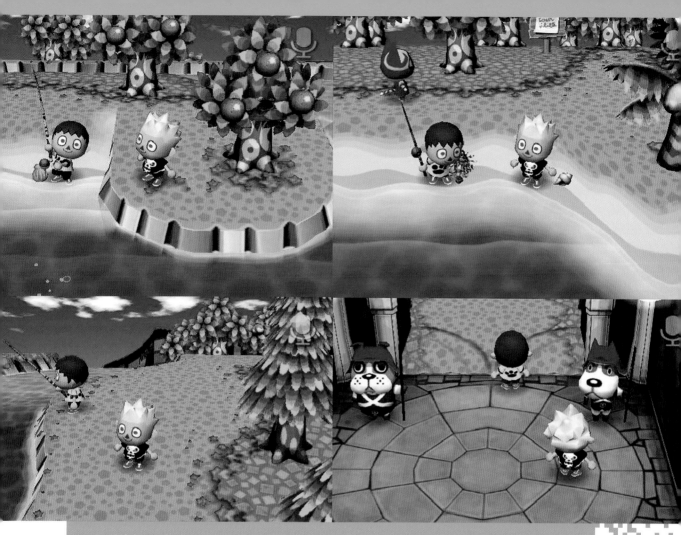

A visiting character uses a fishing rod in *Animal Crossing: City Folk*.
Wii controllers could also be used to move *City Folk* characters
through towns and to draw clothing or wallpaper designs.

instead of *City Folk*. Fans hoped that future *Animal Crossing*
games would be made for handheld **consoles**.

NEW LEAF

In 2013, Nintendo released *Animal Crossing: New Leaf* for the Nintendo 3DS, a handheld **console**. *New Leaf* was the new *Animal Crossing* game players were waiting for. Fans loved that they could play the game anywhere.

New Leaf had a new twist. Players were the mayors of their towns, allowing them to **customize** their towns. In previous games, town layouts were **generated** by computer. But as mayor, a player chose where to place buildings and other structures. By earning and spending Bells, players could also bring new businesses and **amenities** to their towns. These included a café, a lighthouse, and water fountains!

New Leaf had other new features. Players could customize the outsides of their homes. The game also had new residents and clothes, and it recognized more holidays. In addition, players could travel to an island to play mini games with other *New Leaf* players.

A Nintendo DS sits atop an *Animal Crossing: New Leaf* display at a gaming event. *New Leaf* was released in Japan in 2012. It sold 800,000 copies in the first week!

New Leaf players could also upload a copy of their dream town to a **database** called the Dream Suite. This allowed other players to visit the dream town's copy. By 2018, *New Leaf* became the best-selling *Animal Crossing* game yet!

SPIN-OFF SERIES

Thanks to *New Leaf*'s popularity, Nintendo released **spin-off** *Animal Crossing* games in the next years. The first was *Happy Home Designer*, a 2015 game for the 3DS. In this game, players designed home and office interiors based on requests from *Animal Crossing*'s residents.

Players could buy Amiibo cards to use in the game. Amiibos were character figurines that could be wirelessly connected to gameplay. When swiped over the 3DS, the cards added new residents to the game. Many fans enjoyed *Happy Home Designer*. But some missed gathering items and having a home of their own.

Another spin-off game, *Amiibo Festival*, was released for the Nintendo Wii U in 2015. *Amiibo Festival* was a party board game. Players moved Amiibos around a game board and earned or lost "Happy Points."

Amiibo Festival came with two Amiibos and three Amiibo cards. Players used the figurines to play as those characters in the game. They used the cards to play mini games.

Unfortunately, *Amiibo Festival* was not popular with fans or critics. Many felt the Amiibos were cute. However, they also felt the gameplay was boring.

In addition to Amiibo cards (*bottom right*), Nintendo sold *Happy Home Designer* themed cover plates (*left*) for the Nintendo 3DS.

POCKET CAMP

After *Amiibo Festival*'s poor reviews, Nintendo decided to take *Animal Crossing* in a new direction. An *Animal Crossing* mobile game, *Pocket Camp*, was released for smartphones in 2017.

Instead of living in houses, *Pocket Camp* characters lived at campsites. They talked to and fulfilled requests for residents at nearby recreation areas. In addition to Bells, characters could earn materials such as wood to make furniture. Making certain pieces of furniture allowed players to invite nearby residents to stay at their campsites.

Fans liked *Pocket Camp* at first. However, **updates** to the game were unpopular. For example, the original version allowed players to earn Leaf Tickets by completing in-game goals. They could use the tickets to unlock furniture and characters. However, game updates made these goals more difficult to achieve. Players could purchase Leaf Tickets with real money. But many players did not want to pay for in-game rewards.

Nintendo released frequent updates to *Pocket Camp* in the years following its release. These updates added new features, animals, in-game events, and more.

Many longtime *Animal Crossing* fans were disappointed by *Pocket Camp*. Instead, fans continued to play *New Leaf* and hope Nintendo would release a new *Animal Crossing* game.

NEW HORIZONS

In March 2020, *Animal Crossing* fans got their wish. *Animal Crossing*: *New Horizons* **debuted** that month for the Nintendo Switch. The Switch was both a home **console** and a handheld one. So, players could once again take their games on the go!

New Horizons introduced several firsts to the series. Instead of starting in a town, each player moved to a **desert island**. Adding buildings and other **amenities** attracted villagers to the island. As the island's number of amenities and villagers grew, its rating could increase from one to five stars.

As in *Pocket Camp*, players could make new tools and furniture by gathering certain materials. *New Horizons* also allowed players to move buildings. Once an island earned three stars, the player could change its landscape. Adding hills, waterfalls, cliffs, and more made each player's island **unique**. Fans loved *New Horizons*. In just 5 months, the game sold more than 22 million copies!

Shortly after *New Horizons* debuted, the COVID-19 pandemic swept the globe. People wore face masks to avoid contracting and spreading the respiratory disease. Mirroring real life, *New Horizons* offerings included in-game face masks for characters.

9

DESIGNING RESIDENTS

Animal Crossing fans love interacting with the game's many animal residents. In *New Horizons*, there are 35 resident species and more than 400 **unique** resident characters. How do the games' designers create each one?

First, designers select an animal **silhouette**. Each species in the game has one silhouette. This is so a player can recognize a species even from a distance. Species include cats, hippos, alligators, and dogs.

Designers work to make each character's appearance different within its silhouette. They do this by changing elements such as colors, markings, facial features, and clothing.

Each animal is then given a personality. In *New Horizons*, there are eight different personality types. They influence how a character interacts with players and other residents.

Animal Crossing residents on Amiibo cards. In addition to unique clothing and features, game designers give each resident a name.

Midge
3/12

Kabuki   Kabuki
11/29

069
Belle   Bella   Prity
12/28
069-CT-ADE

086
Chef   Chief   Zoilo
12/19
086-DK-ADE

02
Salami   Rasher   Curtis
4/7
029-DD-ADE

23

LEVEL UP!

Old and New

New Horizons was a hit with fans. It was the best-selling *Animal Crossing* game so far. In 2020, *New Horizons* was also the second best-selling Switch game of all time.

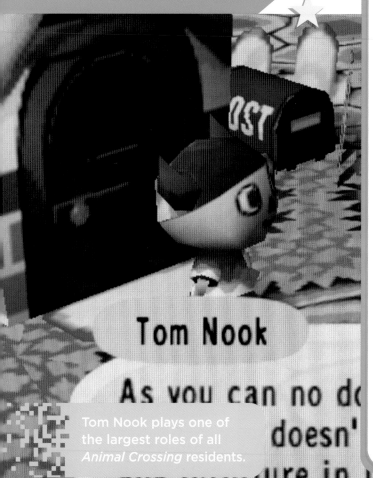

Tom Nook

As you can no do doesn'
any furniture in it at all.

Tom Nook plays one of the largest roles of all *Animal Crossing* residents.

2001 (Japan), **2002** (US)

ANIMAL CROSSING

+ **Console**: Nintendo GameCube

+ Residents: 236, including Tom Nook the raccoon and Mr. Resetti the mole

+ Bug types: 40

+ Fish types: 40

+ **Customizable** clothing: Shirts and hats

+ Gameplay:
  - Players start as residents of small towns.
  - Up to four players can live in the same town, but only one player can play at a time.

ANIMAL CROSSING: NEW HORIZONS

Console: Nintendo Switch

Residents: More than 400, including Raymond the cat and Sherb the goat

Bug types: 80

Fish types: 80

Customizable clothing: Shirts, hats, glasses, pants, dresses, and more

Gameplay:

Players start the game living on **desert islands**.

Up to eight players can live on one island, and up to four can play together at the same time.

Each day in *New Horizons* holds the chance of a special visitor coming to a player's island.

LASTING LEGACY

Nearly 20 years after its first release, *Animal Crossing*'s popularity remained strong. Each month, Nintendo released free *New Horizons* **updates**. Many were based around holidays and seasons. For example, an update in summer 2020 let players swim and catch new sea life. October 2020 brought a Halloween update allowing players to collect candy!

Players looked forward to future updates and new *Animal Crossing* games. The game's developers believed the series would continue to grow and change. However, the core of the *Animal Crossing* games would remain the fun, peaceful life **simulations** that fans loved.

PANDEMIC PLAYING

In 2020, the COVID-19 **pandemic** changed life around the world. Many people stayed at home to avoid spreading or catching the disease. The pandemic also made people feel **anxious**. Playing *New Horizons* gave many gamers something to do while at home. It also helped some people cope with feeling anxious.

Animal Crossing lets gamers enter the virtual world of the games' animal residents. And franchise merchandise allows fans to bring their favorite residents into the real world!

TIMELINE

1986

Eguchi moves to Kyoto, Japan, to work for Nintendo. Feelings of loneliness after the move inspire him to come up with the idea for a life simulation game.

2002

Animal Crossing is released for the GameCube in the United States.

1965

Animal Crossing creator Katsuya Eguchi is born in Tokyo, Japan.

2005

Animal Crossing: Wild World is released for the Nintendo DS.

2001

In April, *Animal Forest* is released for the Nintendo 64 in Japan.

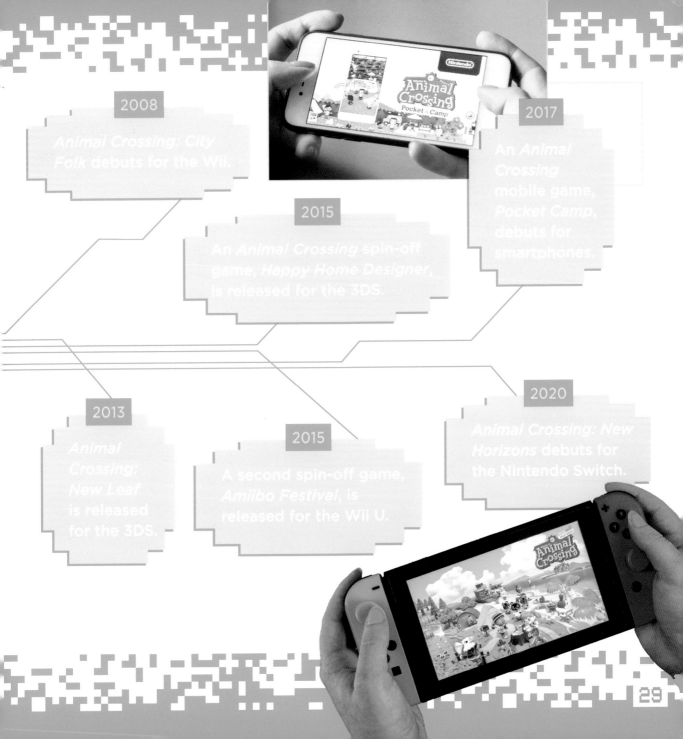

2008

Animal Crossing: City Folk debuts for the Wii.

2015

An *Animal Crossing* spin-off game, *Happy Home Designer*, is released for the 3DS.

2017

An *Animal Crossing* mobile game, *Pocket Camp*, debuts for smartphones.

2013

Animal Crossing: New Leaf is released for the 3DS.

2015

A second spin-off game, *Amiibo Festival*, is released for the Wii U.

2020

Animal Crossing: New Horizons debuts for the Nintendo Switch.

GLOSSARY

accessory—an optional part that adds to the beauty, convenience, or effectiveness of something.

amenity—something that brings comfort, convenience, or enjoyment.

anxious—having an extreme uneasiness of mind or being worried.

console—an electronic system used to play video games.

custom—one of a kind, or made to order. Something that is made to order is customized.

database—a large collection of information.

debut (DAY-byoo)—to first appear. A first appearance is a debut.

desert island—an island where no people live.

franchise—a series of related works, such as movies or video games, that feature the same characters.

generate—to create or produce something.

pandemic—an outbreak of a disease that affects multiple countries and a significant proportion of the population.

portable—able to be carried easily.

random—lacking a definite plan or pattern.

silhouette (sih-luh-WEHT)—the shape or outline of something.

simulation—something that is made to look, feel, or behave like something else.

spin-off—something that imitates or is inspired by an earlier work or product.

unique (yoo-NEEK)—being the only one of its kind.

update—a more modern or up-to-date form of something.

upgraded—having increased or improved quality.

virtual—existing only on computers or on the Internet.

ONLINE RESOURCES

To learn more about *Animal Crossing*, please visit **abdobooklinks.com** or scan this QR code. These links are routinely monitored and updated to provide the most current information available.

INDEX